my little treasury

First Prayers and Blessings

pi kids phoenix international publications, inc.

Cover illustrated by Steve Whitlow

Illustrated by Lisa Alderson, Linda Clearwater, Marina Fedotova, Agnieszka Jatkowska,
Dubravka Kolanovic, Tammie Lyon, Judith Pfeiffer, Sanja Rescek, Janet Samuel, Tish Tenud, and Steve Whitlow

Phoenix International Publications, Inc.
8501 West Higgins Road   59 Gloucester Place
Chicago, Illinois 60631   London W1U 8JJ

Permission is never granted for commercial purposes.

www.pikidsmedia.com

pi kids is a trademark of Phoenix International Publications, Inc.,
and is registered in the United States.

8 7 6 5 4 3 2 1

ISBN: 978-1-4508-7299-7

Table of Contents

This is the day that the Lord has made,
let us rejoice and be glad in it.

Psalm 118:24

Blessings for
the Brand-New Day

Rise and shine and
   give God the glory, glory!
Rise and shine and
   give God the glory, glory!
Rise and shine and
   give God the glory, glory!
Children of the Lord!

O God, creator of light,
at the rising of the sun this morning,
let the greatest of all light,
your love,
rise like the sun within our hearts.

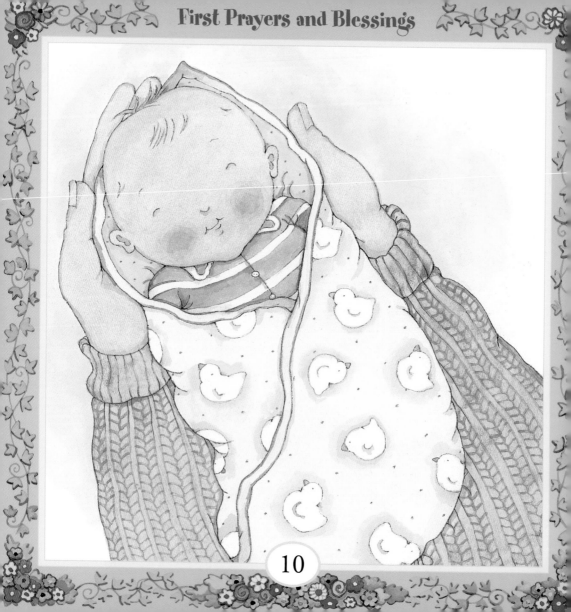

I am small,
my heart is strong;
let no one dwell in it,
except God alone.

Lord, be with me today,
and help me in all I think,
and do,
and say.

Lord, teach us to pray.

13

14

For this new morning and its light,
  for rest and shelter of the night,
For health and food, for love and friends,
  for every gift your goodness sends,
We thank you, gracious Lord.

Good morning, Lord!

Be with me all day long,
until the shadows lengthen,
and the evening comes,
and the busy day is done,
and those at work are back at home.

Then in your mercy,
grant us safe lodging,
a restful mind,
and peaceful sleep.

Do all the good you can,
in all the ways you can,
in all the places you can,
at all the times you can,
for all the people you can,
as long as ever you can.

Dear God, as we start this day,
     please guide us.
Please help Mom and Dad as they work.
Please help me at school.
Please help my brothers and sisters,
     and all my friends and family.

21

Dear Lord, I have a busy day today.

Help me do my chores with cheer
and be kind to others,
even if they are not kind to me.

Watch over me as I go to school
and play with my friends.
Lord, I have a busy day.

Thank you for being by my side.

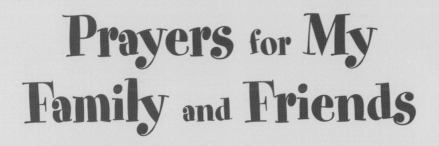

Prayers for My Family and Friends

Peace be to this house
and to all who dwell in it.

Peace be to all who enter
and to all who depart.

Dear God, please take care of my family.
Keep them healthy and safe from harm.
I love them very much.

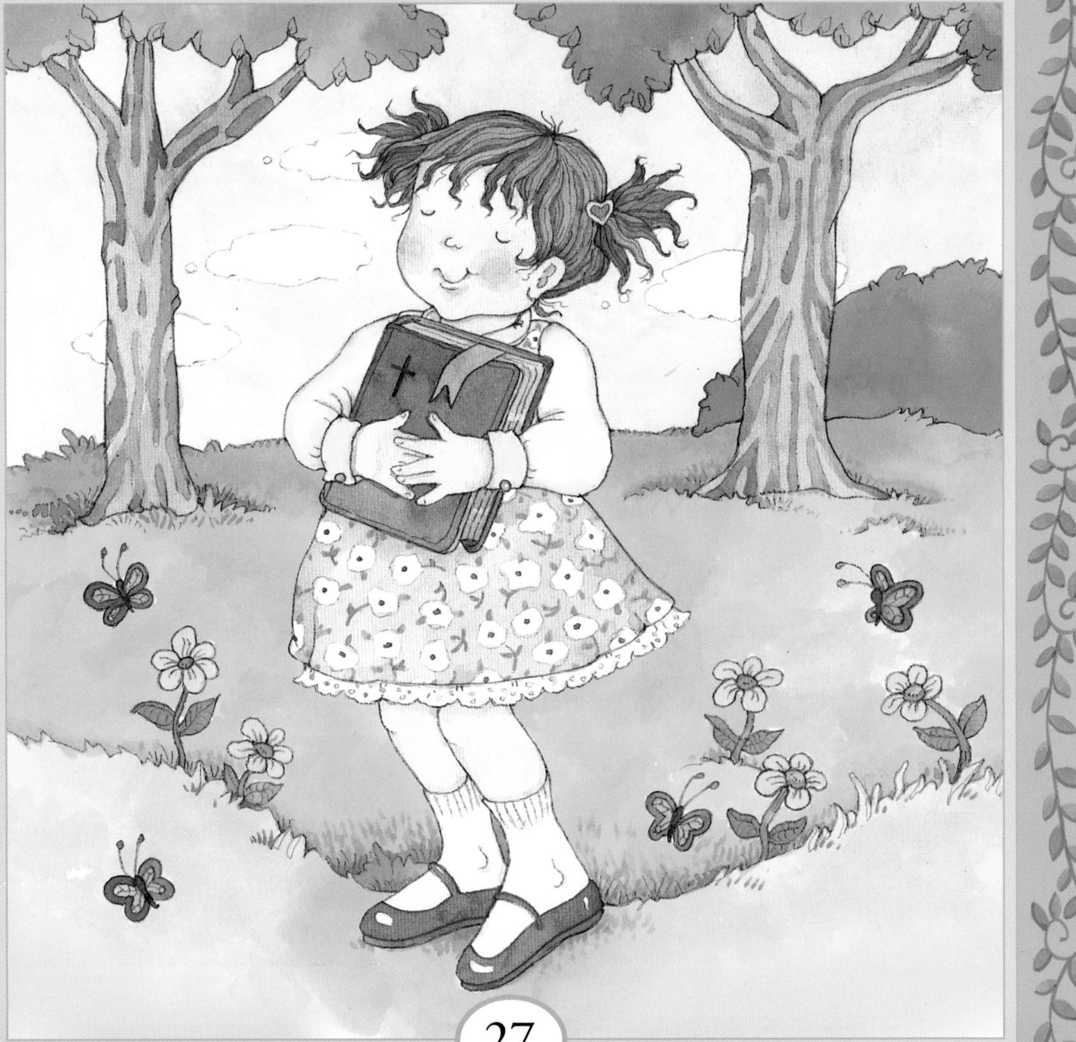

I know that as I grow bigger
my love for my mother and father
grows bigger, too.

Thank you, Lord, for my parents.

Dear God, my parents work very hard
to bring me the things I need.

Please help me to do my part
so that together we are happy
and healthy and safe.

Dear Lord, thank you for my brother.

He is fun to be around
and he looks out for me.

He has good ideas and
he helps me when I need it.

Please know, Lord,
that I treasure my brother.

Dear God, thank you for my sister.

She plays nicely, taking turns.
She likes to go on adventures with me.
And she is kind to everyone.

She is the best sister in the world.
Thank you, God, for my sister.

Prayers for My Family and Friends

35

Dear God, thank you for my grandparents.

My grandma and grandpa have time to spend with me, sharing stories and hugs and kisses.

I know that they love me.

Dear Lord, please be sure that my family knows that I love them very much, even during the times I may not show it.

Lord, teach me the ways of friendship
so that I may be a good friend
to someone who needs me.

Thank you for my friend next door,
   and my friend across the street,
And please help me to be a friend
   to everyone I meet.

43

My friend is special to me.
Lord, please help me to
keep her in my heart until we grow old.

May the road rise to meet you,
    may the wind be always at your back,
May the sun shine warm on your face,
    the rain fall softly on your fields;
And until we meet again,
    may God hold you in the palm of his hand.

Lord, help me never to judge another
until I have walked many miles
in her shoes.

God bless all those who I love.
God bless all those who love me.
God bless all those who love those who I love,
    and all those who love those who love me.

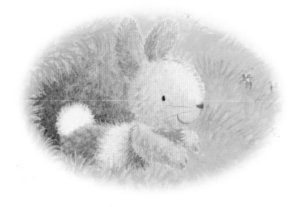

Bless This Food

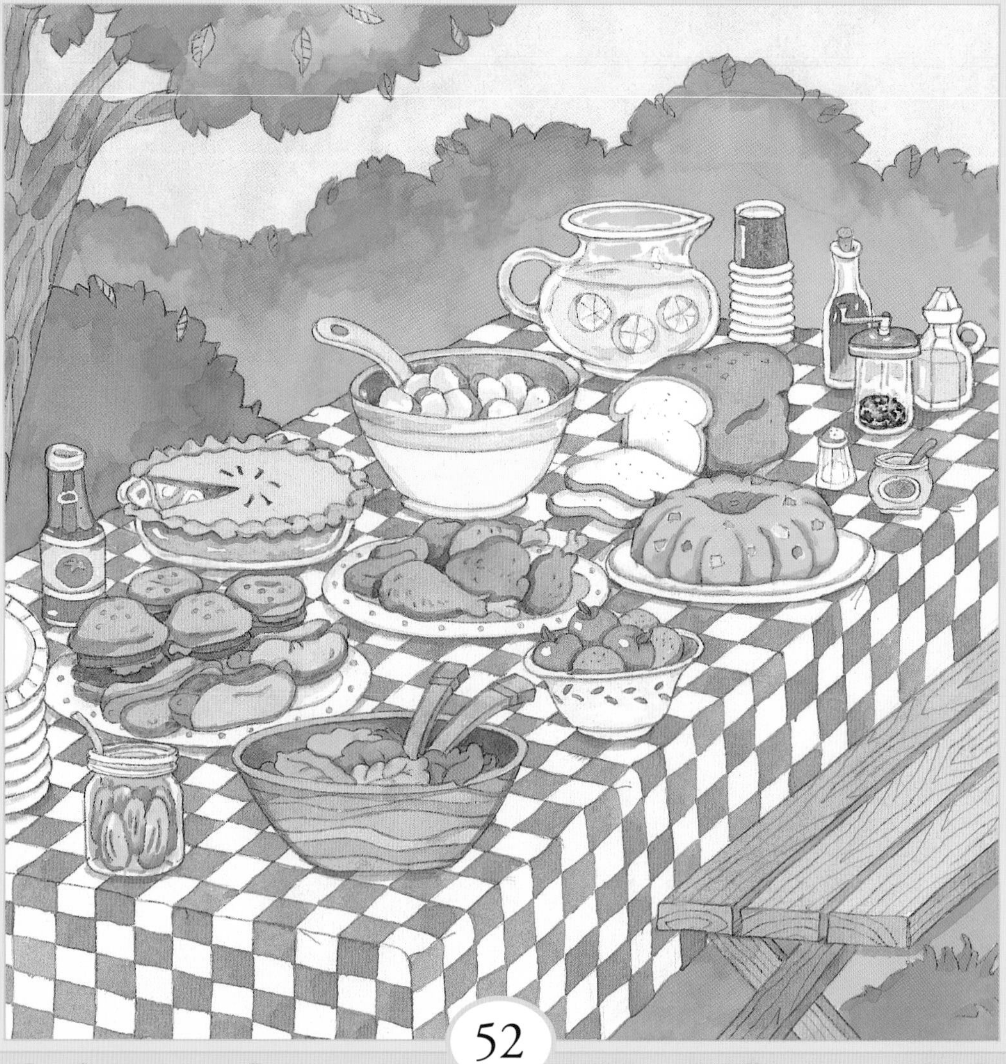

Our hands we fold,
  our heads we bow,
For food and drink,
  we thank God now.

We thank you, Lord,
    for happy hearts,
For rain and sunny weather;

We thank you, Lord,
    for this, our food,
And that we are together.

God is great, God is good,
and we thank God for our food.

Come, O Lord, be our guest.
Let these gifts to us be blessed.

60

Let us in peace eat the food
that God has provided for us.

Praise be to God for all these gifts.
Amen.

Thank you for the world so sweet,
thank you for the food we eat.
Thank you for the birds that sing,
thank you, God, for everything.

For every cup and plateful,
God, make us truly grateful!

Each time we eat,
may we remember God's love.

68

God bless us, every one!

— Charles Dickens

Thank you, O Lord, for these, your gifts,
which we are about to receive from your bounty.

Amen.

Thank You, God

Lord, you know that I love you.

Lord, help us listen to your voice.

Help us to be willing and quick
to do your work.

Help us to be friendly and loving.

And help us to thank you every day
for all your gifts to us.

75

The Lord's Prayer
Our Father, who art in heaven,
    hallowed be thy name.
Thy kingdom come,
    thy will be done, on earth
As it is in heaven.

Give us this day our daily bread;
    and forgive us our trespasses,
As we forgive those who trespass against us;
    and lead us not into temptation,
But deliver us from evil.

For thine is the kingdom,
    and the power, and the glory,
For ever and ever.

                    Amen.

78

Lord,

Grant me a simple, kind, open, believing, loving, and generous heart, worthy of being your dwelling place.

— John Sergieff

79

Dear God, lead me day by day,
  ever in your own sweet way;
Teach me to be pure and true;
  show me what I ought to do.

When in danger, make me brave;
  make me know that you can save;
Keep me safe by your dear side;
  let me in your love abide.

When I'm tempted to do wrong,
	make me steady, wise, and strong;
And when all alone I stand,
	shield me with your mighty hand.
											Amen.

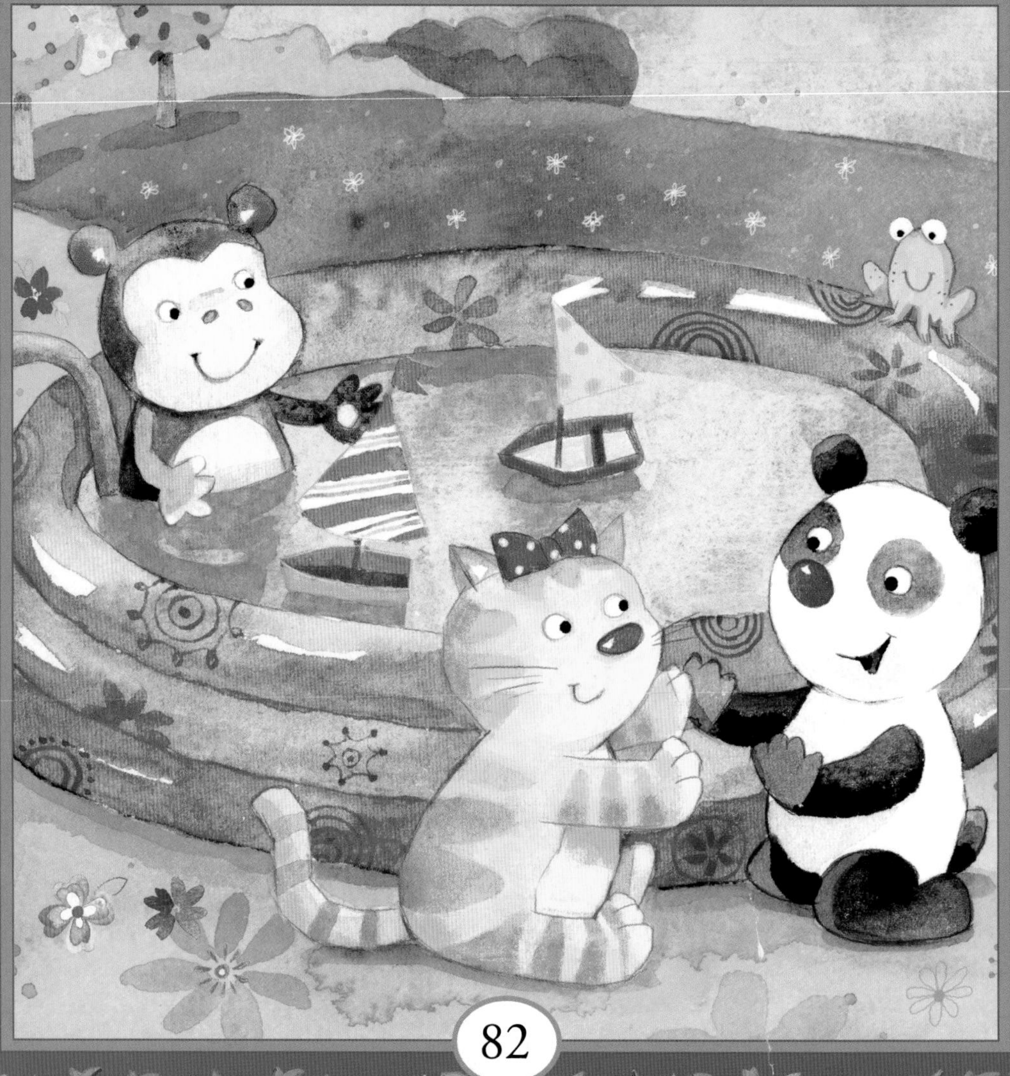

Dear God, be good to me.

The sea is so wide,
and my boat is so small.

All for you, dear God,
everything I do, or think, or say,
the whole day long.

Help me to be good.

Lord, help me to win if I may,
and if I may not,
help me to lose gracefully.

Lord of the loving heart,
    may mine be loving, too.
Lord of the gentle hands,
    may mine be gentle, too.
Lord of the willing feet,
    may mine be willing, too.
So may I grow more like you
    in all I say and do.

89

Dear God, teach this child to pray,
and then accept my prayer.
You hear all the words I say,
for you are everywhere.

Be thou my guardian and my guide,
and hear me when I call;
Let not my slippery footsteps slide,
and hold me lest I fall.

Prayers for **Our World**

93

For crunchy apples, juicy plums,
    and yellow pears so sweet,
For ripened berries on the vine,
    and flowers at our feet,
For ears of corn, and greenest grass,
    and colored leaves on trees,
We thank you, heavenly God above,
    for such good gifts as these.

I never saw a moor,
    I never saw the sea;
Yet know I how the heather looks,
    and what a wave must be.

I never spoke with God,
    nor visited in heaven;
Yet certain am I of the spot
    as if the chart were given.

— Emily Dickinson

When the weather is wet,
  we must not fret.
When the weather is cold,
  we must not scold.
When the weather is warm,
  we must not storm.
Be thankful together,
  whatever the weather.

God made the sun,
    and God made the trees.
God made the mountains,
    and God made me.

Thank you, O God,
    for the sun and the trees,
For making the mountains,
    and for making me.

101

A tiny egg is about to hatch
while a mother bluebird waits
to meet her baby for the first time.

Thank you, God, for nature's miracles.

All things bright and beautiful,
   all creatures great and small,
All things wise and wonderful,
   the Lord God made them all.

— Cecil Frances Alexander

106

Elephants with long gray trunks,
   and teeny-tiny striped chipmunks,
Birds that fly for miles and miles,
   and scaly smiling crocodiles,
Puppies and snug kittens, too,
   and even silly cockatoos,
God shares his wondrous love with all,
   every creature great and small.

Hear my prayer, almighty God,
for our friends the animals.

Give to them all your mercy and pity,
and all compassion from those who deal
with them.

Make all hands that touch them gentle,
and all voices that speak to them kind.

Help us to be true friends to animals,
so that we may all share your blessings.

110

You are to me, O Lord,
what wings are to the flying bird.

Almighty God, hear and bless
all beasts and singing birds.
And guard with tenderness
small things that have no words.

113

God bless the field and bless the lane,
stream and branch and lion's mane,
Bless the minnow and bless the whale,
bless the rainbow and the hail,
Bless the wing and bless the fin,
bless the air I travel in,
Bless the earth and bless the sea,
God bless you and God bless me.

For the beauty of the earth,
  for the glory of the skies,
For the love, which from our birth,
  over and around us lies:
Heavenly God, to you we raise
  this, our hymn of grateful praise.
                              Amen.

Teach Me, Lord

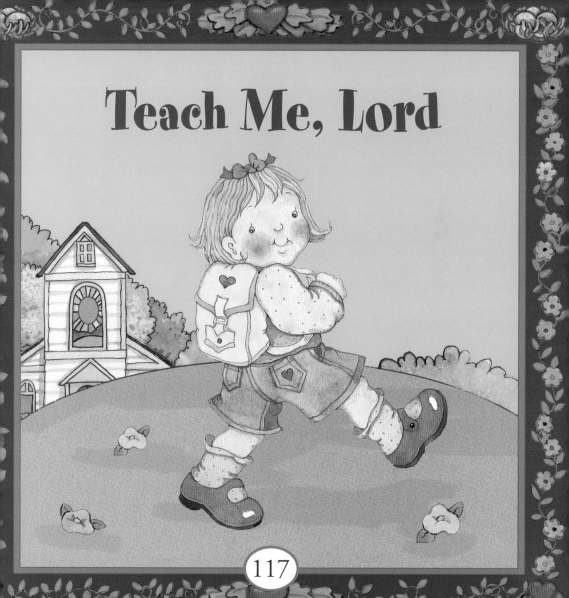

To do to others as I would
    that they should do to me,
Will make me gentle, kind, and good,
    as everyone should be.

Lord, you are in everything I do.
    My words and thoughts are touched by you.
When I'm in a time of need,
    my prayers I send to you with speed.

120

121

Dear Lord, please give me what I ask,
   if you'd be glad about it.
But if you think it's not for me,
   please help me do without it.

Every day you bring us joy,
 for every girl and every boy.
In each and every friendship, too,
 we feel the strength and love of you.
Lord, how you touch our lives,
 our faith and love keep us alive.

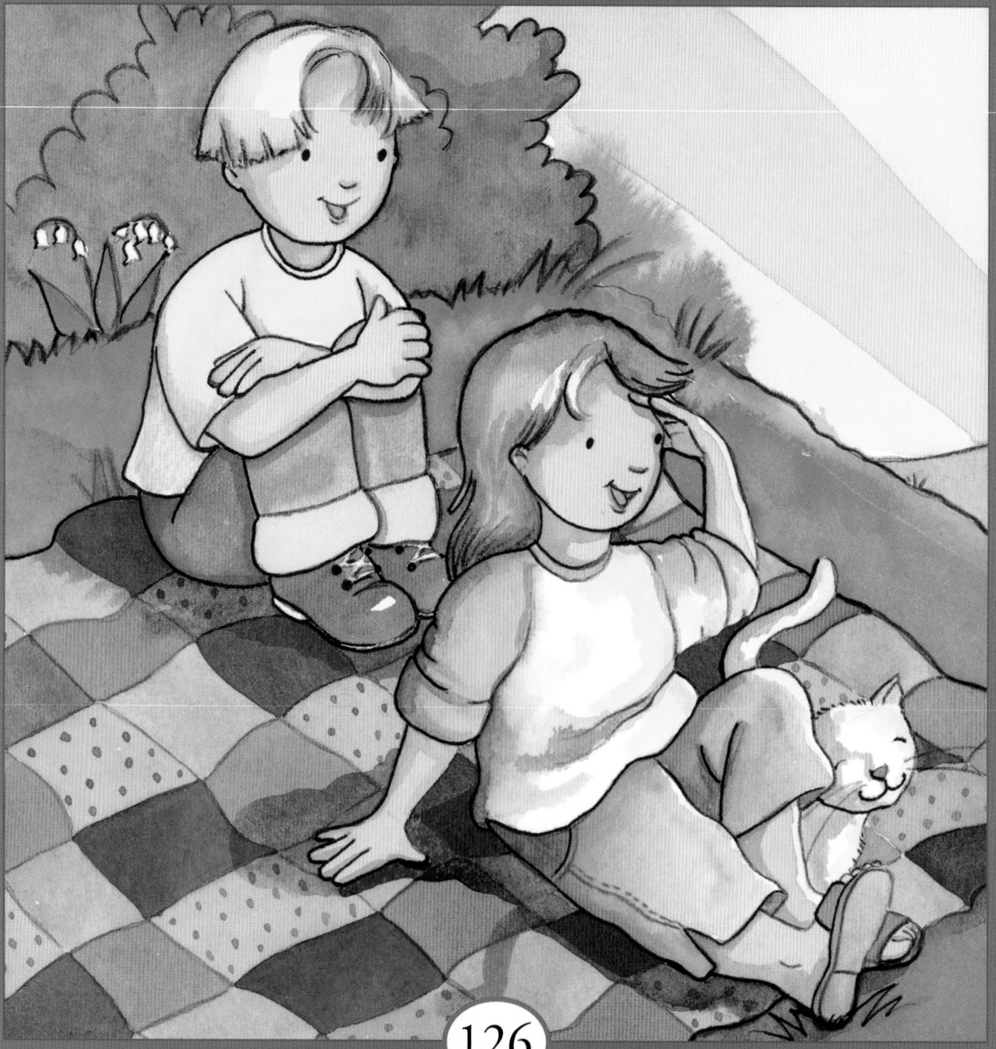

God is light, and in him is no darkness at all.

Praise God for every child,
as each one's different and each one's special.

May each child know God's love,
and share that love with one another.

May each child look at the other,
and not see "different," but "brother."

129

What can I give him,
   poor as I am?
If I were a shepherd,
   I would bring a lamb;
If I were a wise man,
   I would do my part;
Yet what can I give him:
   give my heart.

— Christina Rossetti

Little drops of water,
     little grains of sand,
Make the mighty ocean,
     and the pleasant land.

Thus the little minutes,
     humble though they be,
Make the mighty ages
     of eternity.

Little deeds of kindness,
little words of love,
Make this earth an Eden,
like the heaven above.

— Isaac Watts

134

God is Love, and we are his children.
There is no room for fear in love.
We love because he loved us first.

To you, O Lord,
I lift up my soul.

Psalm 24:1

136

Good-Night Prayers

138

Good night,
  sleep tight,
Wake up bright
  in the morning light
To do what's right
  with all my might.

Now the day is over,
    night is drawing nigh.
Shadows of the evening
    steal across the sky.

Now the darkness gathers,
    stars begin to peep.
Birds and beasts and flowers
    soon will be asleep.

Dear God, give the weary
calm and sweet repose;
With your tender blessing,
soon our eyes will close.

142

Now I lay me down to sleep,
   I pray the Lord my soul to keep.
Your love stay with me through the night,
   and wake me with the morning light.

143

Lord, stay by my side tonight,
    now that day is done.
May angels comfort me in sleep,
    until the morning sun.

144

146

I hear no voice, I feel no touch,
  I see no glory bright;
But yet I know that God is near,
  in darkness as in light.

I see the moon,
    and the moon sees me.
God bless the moon,
    and God bless me.

149

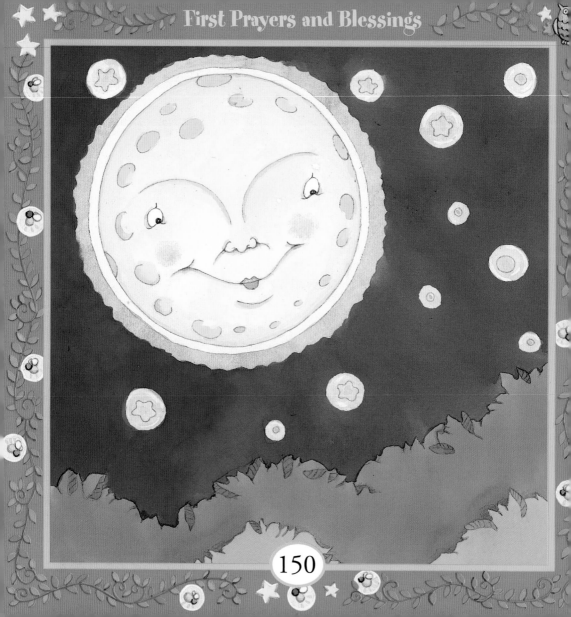

The moon shines bright,
the stars give light,
Before the break of day;

God bless you all,
both great and small,
And send a joyful day.

Day is done.
Gone the sun
from the lakes,
from the hills,
from the sky.

All is well,
safely rest.
God is nigh.

154

I will lie down and sleep in peace,
knowing you, O Lord,
watch over me.

Good night! Good night!
Far flies the light;
But still God's love
shall flame above,
Making all bright.
Good night! Good night!

—Victor Hugo

157

The Lord is all I need.
He takes care of me.

Psalm 16:5

God is near to every one of us.
In God, we live and move and grow.